Lord Break My Heart

I Died When God Broke My Heart

Priscilla H. Penn

WESTBOW
PRESS®
A DIVISION OF THOMAS NELSON
& ZONDERVAN

Scripture taken from the King James Version of the Bible.

This book is a work of non-fiction. Unless otherwise noted, the author
and the publisher make no explicit guarantees as to the accuracy of
the information contained in this book and in some cases, names of
people and places have been altered to protect their privacy.

WestBow Press books may be ordered through booksellers or by contacting:

WestBow Press
A Division of Thomas Nelson & Zondervan
1663 Liberty Drive
Bloomington, IN 47403
www.westbowpress.com
1 (866) 928-1240

Because of the dynamic nature of the Internet, any web addresses or
links contained in this book may have changed since publication and
may no longer be valid. The views expressed in this work are solely those
of the author and do not necessarily reflect the views of the publisher,
and the publisher hereby disclaims any responsibility for them.

Any people depicted in stock imagery provided by Thinkstock are
models, and such images are being used for illustrative purposes only.
Certain stock imagery © Thinkstock.

ISBN: 978-1-5127-7323-1 (sc)
ISBN: 978-1-5127-7324-8 (e)

Library of Congress Control Number: 2017901156

Print information available on the last page.

WestBow Press rev. date: 02/08/2017

Contents

Dedication

I dedicate this book to Mamzel H. Clark, my grandmother, whose life inspired me to seek to know God on the deepest level possible. She was the most courageous, consistent, and consecrated person I've ever known. I will always be grateful for her sacrifice in raising me. My desire has always been to make it all worthwhile.

I dedicate this book as well to my husband, Timothy, whose devotion to me is unparalleled. I am known for making up words, but I can't make up one to describe this man. He provided everything I needed to complete this book. Thank you, honey. I pray you know how much I appreciate your support in everything I do.

Foreword

L *ord, Break My Heart* is timeless but very critical to this dispensation of bitterness and social, political, and spiritual unrest. Penn captures this subject with total transparency by aligning her betterment to the brokenness spanning critical times of her early life up to and including ministry.

She prepared a sermon without knowing that it captured her story then transformed it into a life benefit for others. This work impressively examines how life's contributions contribute to the inner heart and shape the good and bad in our lives.

Penn uses the subject Lord, break my heart eloquently to show how the creator of life is able to create clean hearts and renew right spirits in us. This is a must-read for anyone who has undergone disappointment, peril, or personal affronts. Freedom awaits you in this book, for those whom the Son sets free are completely free.

Lord, Break My Heart contains answers along with keys to love, liberty, and life.

Dr. Andrew Carnegie Turner II
Certified Professional Executive Level Life Coach, Author, Leader
September 2016

Introduction

This book is not meant to bash anyone or glorify me but to glorify God and honor the truth of His Word. I received inspiration to write this book in a message the Lord gave me to deliver at a Women's Day Service in 2011. All Scripture quotation are taken from KJV - King James Version. My subject derived from: (Psalms 51:17). "The sacrifices of God are a broken spirit: a broken and a contrite heart, O God, thou wilt not despise." My subject: Lord, break my heart!

Saying those words aloud made me acutely aware that it wasn't just a title for a sermon but rather a request. I began trying to discover when and if I had allowed the Lord to completely break my heart. Certainly, there had to be a measure of breaking and belief in God for salvation because the Word says, "But without faith it is impossible to please him: for he that cometh to God must believe that he is, and that he is a rewarder of them that diligently seek him" (Hebrews 11:6). However, I felt deeply that there was more work to be done in me.

The Lord penetrated my heart for repentance for me to be saved; for if you had met me before salvation ... ummm. I was only fourteen when the Lord saved me, but I thought I was a horrible person because I had no love in my heart until God filled me with Himself.

But even after we're saved, we still need God's assistance in the other areas of our lives. We may attend Bible study, church services, conventions, and prayer meetings, but who takes time to break the Word down to where it talks about basic relationships (how to get along with everybody), marriage, raising children, ministry, and so on? If you don't realize you need Him in every area of your life, not just for salvation, you'll flounder around trying to figure out *Why can't I get this or that right?*

My initial breaking was at salvation, but I needed more breaking. I had not one or two levels of stuff but piles and piles of trauma and drama. I invite you to walk with me through my experiences as the Lord continued to break my heart in various areas of my life. You will not understand the areas in your life that need breaking unless you allow the Holy Spirit to show you yourself. This happens when you make a habit of obeying the Word, which admonishes us to "Pray without ceasing" (1 Thessalonians 1:17). The Holy Spirit, the master teacher, will teach you how to be an obedient child, a godly friend, a godly spouse, leader, or whatever the Lord has called you to be. How can you be taught if you're not aware of what in your life needs fixing?

At every interval of your walk with the Lord, ask Him to break your heart so He can take out your preconceived ideas and notions and place in you what He desires you to know to fit every situation. Reliance on the Lord alone is key! "Then shall we know, if we follow on to know the LORD: his going forth is prepared as the morning; and he shall come unto us as the rain, as the latter and former rain unto the earth" (Hosea 6:3). "Trust in the LORD with all thine heart; and lean not unto thine own understanding. In all thy ways acknowledge him, and he shall direct thy paths" (Proverbs 3:5–6). "The heart is deceitful above all things, and desperately wicked: who can know it?" (Jeremiah 17:9).

I've preached many messages since I began in 1992, but none has stuck with me as much as has "Lord, break my heart." The Lord impressed upon my heart and mind to quit working on the book I was working on and to write this book. He said to me, "I need my people to know that if they don't allow me to completely break their hearts, they will never be free of the hurt, pain, unforgiveness, etc. Consequently, they will never know how to become the kingdom citizens I have called them to be. For how could they help deliver those souls who are steeped in hurt, deceit, pain, unforgiveness, etc. if they have not been delivered?"

When we surrender our hearts to the Lord, He will clean them out and replace them with His heart, a heart of flesh. "A new heart also will I give you, and a new spirit will I put within you: and I will take away the stony heart out of your flesh, and I will give you an heart of flesh" (Ezekiel 36:26). When our hearts are emptied of the debris we were born with as well as the misery life has thrust upon us, we can become whom God has ordained us to be. Since we had no say in how we came into the world, we must accept how God allowed us to enter;

for the most part, it will be the platform from which we will minister (and I'm not just talking from behind a pulpit). Our effectiveness will come from our experiences and encounters with Him. That's why we must ask Him to break our hearts. "Create in me a clean heart, O God; and renew a right spirit within me" (Psalm 51:10).

A clean heart and a right spirit are the criteria for kingdom ministry. Many times, we want to advance in the kingdom but can't seem to move forward. So we ask, *What or who is hindering me?* Well, we hinder ourselves. My desire is that we deliberately search our hearts to see if we have allowed them to be broken by the Lord, to see if we have truly died! "Verily, verily, I say unto you, Except a corn of wheat fall into the ground and die, it abideth alone: but if it die, it bringeth forth much fruit" (John 12:24).

My story will shed light on the areas we should work on so we can bring forth much fruit.

CHAPTER 1

Humble Beginnings

How do we begin to search our hearts to determine whether we've allowed the Lord to break them? I'll start with my humble beginnings though my beginnings were so humble that there's not a whole lot to write about. To this day, they keep me grounded. I've come far by the grace of God, but I remember where I came from; that helps me focus on where I need to go. But I didn't feel that way growing up—quite the contrary.

My earliest memories are from when I was around five. My kindergarten teacher's name was Ms. Brown. Don't know why, but that has always been important to me. I had Ms. Brown up to third grade.

We lived in a three-room house—yes, a three-room house, not a three-bedroom house. We went to the bathroom outside. You ever heard of an outhouse? And we bathed in a washtub and got water from a hydrant outside. My beginnings were indeed humble, but I had the most important thing in my life that would cause me to soar—love. It was hard to realize the gravity of the love at that time due to the anger and confusion I felt.

People would call me mean, but I was broken. I was upset about not being raised by my parents. I couldn't understand it then. My grandmother raised me. I've come to understand why God allowed that. I've paid close attention to those who were raised by their grandparents, especially by their grandmothers. They tend to have an edge over those raised by their parents. This is just my observation, but it's no mystery. There's no way parents can know as much about parenting as grandparents do. They haven't lived long enough to experience what grandparents have. The wisdom and the experiences just aren't there.

I know that it was God's plan for my grandmother to raise me. From her, I learned what it meant to have a relationship with the Lord, and she imparted her wisdom and knowledge to me. Because of her, I am who I am in the body of Christ. I will always appreciate my grandmother because I know she loved me—she was the one constant in my life. She didn't talk love or say, "I love you"; she showed love by her commitment to me. Even today, I don't pay much attention to folk who tell me they love me because love is in action and doesn't stand still. I am still in awe of this woman who gave birth to seventeen children yet was willing to raise me. Because of her, I came to know love because I came to know Jesus. Even my grandmother's love couldn't stand up to the love of God though her love directed me to His love.

The hymn "The Love of God" was written in 1917 by Frederick M. Lehman.

> Oh, love of God, how rich and pure!
> How measureless and strong!
> It shall forevermore endure—
> The saints' and angels' song.

My nephew asked me to sing it at his wedding, but at the time, I hadn't heard of it. I went over it a couple of times a few hours before the wedding. Because of the lyrics and the fact I had literally experienced the love of God, it was as if I just opened my mouth and my heart sang the song. I felt that because by that time in my life, I had truly experienced the love of God and knew firsthand there was nothing like it. It was one of the most amazing experiences of my life.

By the way, when my nephew asked me to sing the song at his wedding, he wasn't even dating anyone. One thing for sure—we are sure the Lord gave him the idea to have that song sung for a reason. Since that time, we all have experienced the benefits of knowing the love of God.

CHAPTER 2

Childhood Memories

My childhood memories are minimal, sort of like my humble beginnings. I basically did only three things: I went to school, I went to church, and I went to the nation's capital to visit my parents and my aunts during my summer breaks and at Christmas. I kept to myself all through school. They called me the Sound of Silence. I figured by staying to myself, I wouldn't have to worry as much about people always asking me about my family (in school as well as in church): "Who are your mother and father?" "Where do they live?" "Why aren't you with them?" I could understand the children asking me those questions, but why the adults? I thought, *I'm just five! Why are you asking me such questions? I'm the child, you're the adult—you figure it out and then tell me!*

Such questions made me painfully aware that I wasn't being raised in a traditional home. But now, I appreciate that I was raised in a godly home. However, those signifying questions would make me even more angry and withdrawn. I am sure that's why I'm so protective of children. I never could understand why adults couldn't sense that children need to be protected from more than just what people call the boogeyman.

To show you how bad it was, can you believe a Sunday school teacher stopped the class when I walked in to ask me, "Is so-and-so your father?" At that time and even today, I wished that nosy, grown folk would have realized how their questions affected young children's lives or even older children's lives for that matter.

I didn't know then that my experiences in life would be the catalyst to bring me to my purpose and my ministry in the kingdom. I know what it feels like not to have things I needed for school or how it feels to be hurt by insensitive adults. Everyone knows children will be cruel to each other, but the anxiety of wondering which adult would inquire next about my family life was exhausting! I'm reminded of the scripture, "For we have not an high priest which cannot be touched with the feeling of our infirmities; but was in all points tempted like as we are, yet without sin" (Hebrews 4:15). Even as early as elementary school, God was instructing me how to handle precarious situations. It was as if He could feel my anxieties when adults around me had no clue.

I didn't realize it at the time, but He knew how I felt and was working it all out for my good. I am in no way comparing my temptations to those our Lord endured, but I can be touched with the feelings of others' infirmities because I've been there. That's why I'm protective of anyone's child, not just my own.

The Lord won't allow you to go through everything there is to go through, but He will allow you to go through those things that will affect you so you can affect someone else. You cannot be as effective if you haven't endured some hard times because the majority of the people you meet grew up under difficult circumstances.

The craziness of my early years helped me understand children and young adults well. I can even understand old folk especially now that I'm old myself. I pray that adults reading this book will please keep their eyes and ears open. I tell them to take notice when children are acting out. Instead of calling them names, ignoring them, or calling them bad, take time to find out what's going on with them. Be discreet about it, and ask the Lord to guide you about what should be done.

I'm thankful something good came out of my pain of humble beginnings and dealing with adults. It taught me to be protective of children. The Lord has used me to be their voice when other adults around them were oblivious. I could pretty much tell by their behavior what they were going through, especially if they were acting out.

My fondest memory was going to church. I preferred being by myself because so I wouldn't have to worry about interacting with ignorant, insensitive folk constantly trying to figure me out. However, I did find solace in fellowship though I rarely said anything to anyone. I hadn't been baptized or received the baptism of the Holy Spirit, but I loved Bible class taught by such gifted and anointed teachers as my pastor Elder John N. Walters, Bishop Samuel Grimes, Bishop Morris E. Golder, and Pastor Ora Schofield. I remember the anointing was so high on Sunday morning that the saints would dance for a couple of hours. Have you ever heard the older saints say they saw fog or a heavy mist in the church? That's the truth. If you haven't experienced it, keep worshiping—you will.

My oldest brother and one of my cousins were a part of our family during the early part of our growing up. They didn't particularly share my enthusiasm for church going, so they would sometimes get upset with me because they knew if I went to church, they had to go as well. I didn't realize at that time that this was the beginning of the Lord preparing me for His kingdom work. He was allowing me to experience everything I would need to effect change in the individuals He allowed to cross my path. How could I ever tell anybody what it felt like to not be in a traditional home with a mother and father if I hadn't gone through it, one of the most painful things I had to endure as a child? Today, it doesn't appear to be such a big deal, but back then, it was horrible.

My parents didn't have a clue about what I was going through because they'd been raised in traditional homes. Does it sound as if I'm trying to bash them? I certainly don't mean to, but if you had asked me that question fifty years ago, you would have gotten a different answer. I'm reminded of the scripture, "When I was a child, I spake as a child, I understood as a child, I thought as a child: but when I became a man, I put away childish things" (1 Corinthians 13:11). I'm trying to give my testimony of how God allowed my heart to be broken so He could fill me with His love, forgiveness, and peace. I desperately needed His love because at a very early age, I experienced hatred and bitterness; it was so bad that I wondered how on earth God would save me. Didn't you have to be able to feel something to be saved? I mean feel something other than a cold and clammy heart filled with hate? My heart was a block of ice. The bitterness, hurt, and pain were almost unbearable. As we often say, "If it hadn't been for the Lord on my side."

"A new heart also will I give you, and a new spirit will I put within you: and I will take away the stony heart out of your flesh, and I will give you an heart of flesh" (Ezekiel 36:26). It's all I can do to contain myself when I read or hear someone quote this scripture. I lived it! How do you think I can tell others that God can heal their broken hearts if I hadn't allowed Him to heal mine?

If your heart is filled with bitterness, unforgiveness, anger, hatred, and abandonment issues, trust me when I tell you all that can be replaced with God's love. I can't even mention God's love without getting all worked up because I vehemently know the difference between His love and a heart full of hatred. Saying it's like night and day is an understatement. He broke my heart you all, and He's still breaking it.

CHAPTER 3

Signs of Change

Allowing your heart to be broken will manifest in your actions. You will see signs that His love has taken root. Your response to unfavorable situations won't cause you to lose it as you had in the past. We as believers don't understand that God's love will automatically exemplify the fruit of the Spirit. When we truly possess it, it will be demonstrated. It will be a part of our daily lives. Our hearts of flesh and the love of God will show up like neon lights! We won't be able to behave differently; believe me.

When you get off course or get in your flesh, the overwhelming spirit of His love will bring you under subjection every time. Whew! I'm feeling it right now, but I can't completely give in to it or I will never finish this book. I mention a little about a heart of flesh at the end of chapter 2, but let's clarify what that means. We will also touch on the love of God vs. humanity's love; those subjects are intertwined.

A Heart of Flesh

Not until God's love takes up residence in your heart will you have a heart of flesh. That can happen only when you allow Him to break your heart. His love couldn't come in and abide in me until I completely let bitterness, anger, and unforgiveness go. No one can feel or know the heart or mind of God until he or she has experienced His love first!

I could not believe it; right before my eyes, I was seeing behavioral changes in me. The first time I witnessed myself not wanting to tear into others for something crazy they said or did was a miracle. In the past, I'd snap even if someone had done nothing. But then, I was beginning to change.

When we feel something other than anger, bitterness, and rage, we notice that. Most of us don't understand that when we strike out at others, there's a hidden sore prompting us to do that. I can still hear myself snapping at people. It took some getting used to hearing my voice sounding kinder and softer when I'd respond to others. *Oh my goodness! What am I feeling? Why does it feel all warm and fuzzy? Is this by chance what the Word calls a heart of flesh?* The demonstration of this miracle was when I could stay in the same room with those who had hurt me deeply; prior to experiencing a God-broken heart, I'd immediately leave the room when they came in.

We're quick to talk about what someone did to us, but rarely if ever do we admit we've hurt others as well. I'm sure some would say they never did or said anything to hurt or offend anyone, but the Word says we all have sinned and come short of the glory of God. That means that even if we didn't mean to or intend to, we have hurt someone. No matter what our intentions are, people have different perceptions and expectations than we do. No matter how hard we try, someone will be hurt or offended. However, it still doesn't mean we shouldn't make every attempt to do our best in treating people right. That doesn't always feel good, but we do it because it's our responsibility. We're accountable to God for ourselves, not to others, so we should never allow others' behavior to dictate how we behave.

The Love of God vs. Man's Love

"Having a form of godliness, but denying the power thereof: from such turn away" (2 Timothy 3:5). I don't know how we can profess to be Bible-believing Christians yet deny the power of God to truly allow us to love as Christ loves. When we don't love as Christ loves, that's called man's love pure and simple. When you can accomplish this, everything else is attainable. And, without the love of God, everything else is futile!

Pay Close Attention

Pay attention here because God's love differs greatly from man's love. You can change only for a time when you experience man's love, but only God's love is everlasting. You'll see the change, and others will as well. Your heart's desire will be to please Him in all things. There will be times when you'll be challenged with whether to please leadership (man's love) or please Him (God's love). I believe in obeying leadership, but when we're faced with complex issues and have to choose between the two, prayer and waiting on direction from Him has always worked for me.

When there is real change in your behavior, you won't flip-flop. The way you act in church, on your job, or at home will be the same. When I was growing up, I saw a difference between the way the saints acted in church and the way they behaved elsewhere. I didn't understand the double life; I couldn't figure out why there was no continuity. Why was the preacher teaching the Word of God, the choir singing the Word, and the saints were testifying about being overcomers? Silly me. I just couldn't get it. I was witnessing pretty much anything you could think of except the love of God.

As always, there were a few real saints who were attempting to live up to their profession, but just as it is today, there were only a few. I guess I was and still am too literal. I believed the Word of God was powerful enough to manifest in us. I was realizing the truth of God's Word in my life, so I knew He was real. Observing the signs of change in my life encouraged me to continue my quest for a broken heart.

I hope by divulging this information, you get some idea of my journey to search out specifically when I allowed God to break my heart and it helps you make a decision to do the same.

CHAPTER 4

God in My Life

I loved going to church as a child, and I still do. God touched my heart in a revival that evangelist Nora Edmunds was running when I was about thirteen. I believe it was in the next service at my home church that my former pastor, Elder John N. Walters, made the altar call. I couldn't believe my legs were carrying me to the altar. My pastor baptized me in the name of the Lord Jesus Christ, and that was the beginning of the change in me. My ice-cold heart hadn't been completely broken, but it had started to melt.

While visiting with my mom and aunts, the Clark sisters, in the summer of 1962, I received the baptism of the Holy Spirit at age fourteen. It was on a Sunday night. I can tell you unequivocally that that experience was the initial breaking of my ice cold heart! I received the gift of the Holy Spirit. It was only a matter of just saying to myself that I would receive the gift now, and I meant it in my heart.

I walked back to the tarrying (waiting) room and tossed my fan in the window. Don't know why it was so important for me to tell that part; I'm sure no one cares. But as I was bending my knee, I received the gift of the Holy Spirit speaking in tongues as the spirit of God gave me utterance. "Then Peter said unto them, Repent, and be baptized every one of you in the name of Jesus Christ for the remission of sins, and ye shall receive the gift of the Holy Ghost" (Acts 2:38).

I had to rend my heart instead of my garment. "And rend your heart, and not your garments, and turn unto the LORD your God: for he is gracious and merciful, slow to anger, and of great kindness, and repenteth him of the evil" (Joel 2:13).

My spiritual birth was the most miraculous thing that has ever happened to me because I really couldn't understand how God could have saved a cold-hearted person like me. I didn't know how He could soften my heart toward Him. When I think about it now, it's tough to keep it together. My spiritual birth is something I'll never get used to; it's what I think about when doubt comes. If God saved me, He can do anything! He can save any human being no matter what he or she has done. Whenever I'd say, "If God saved me, He can save anybody," my mom would ask, "What are you talking about? You sound and act as if you were a cut throat or something." She never knew I had had a heart full of hatred and bitterness; I had never told her. But I didn't feel the need to after the Lord had saved me and the hatred and resentment were gone.

We used to sing "Since Jesus Came into My Heart," which Rufus H. McDaniel wrote in 1914 after the death of his son.

What a wonderful change in my life has been wrought
Since Jesus came into my heart;
I have light in my soul for which long I have sought,
Since Jesus came into my heart.

God did one other very important thing when He filled me with the Holy Spirit—He filled me with instant love for someone I knew I didn't love. I don't know if everyone receives a special healing along with the infilling of the Holy Spirit, but my initial infilling of the Holy Spirit was the beginning of God creating in me a "clean heart" (Psalm 51:10). He filled me with instant love! I had never felt love like that before or since. That's why I know God is truly love.

God filling me with instant love was a phenomenal feeling, but that was just the beginning of death to all the pain and misery in my cold, dark heart. Two scriptures come to mind: "Verily, verily, I say unto you, Except a corn of wheat fall into the ground and die, it abideth alone: but if it die, it bringeth forth much fruit" (John 12:24) and "For ye are dead, and your life is hid with Christ in God" (Colossians 3:3).

I can tell you from experience that dying to self brings forth much good fruit. When my heart was cold and unyielding, I wasn't able to allow God or anyone else to enter it. But after the initial breaking of my heart, I could see things from His vantage point; I could finally see how undone I was and how much I needed to continue to die to my ways, thoughts, and ideas.

Until God filled me with the Holy Spirit, I resented the fact that my parents didn't raise me, but I know now that was the way God allowed it to happen. God knew I would benefit greatly from my grandmother's upbringing. I needed her wisdom and her experience for those things and areas of ministry the Lord wanted me to do.

Concerning the resentment I had toward my parents, I came to understand as an adult that we can do only what we know to do, and unless our consciousness is raised in certain areas of life, we won't know to do things any differently. And the other side of the coin is that the Lord lets certain things happen to us for Him to get the glory out of the situation.

After I received the Holy Spirit, everything started to come together. Debby Boone wrote "You Took My Heart By Surprise"; it best describes what happened to me when the Lord broke my heart.

> Just when I thought my heart had no feeling,
> and life had no music, no rhythm or rhyme,
> you came along, like a warm summer wind,
> you lifted me up, when I needed a friend.

This song spoke to my situation then and now because Jesus took my heart by surprise. The change that came over my cold heart was the most memorable thing that has ever happened to me. Even now, I am deliberately not fully absorbing the event because every time I think about it, I break all over again. I am forever amazed at the grace of God that caught my falling soul. The song "Amazing Grace" by Dottie Rambo speaks to my heart.

Amazing grace shall always be my song of praise
for it was grace that brought my liberty,
I'll never know just how He came to love me so
he looked beyond my faults and saw my need.

Not until you allow Him to break your heart will you be able to completely trust Him. As your trust in Him grows, you'll become willing to surrender your life to Him and realize your purpose on earth.

CHAPTER 5

Marriage

After I graduated from high school, my grandmother and I moved to Washington, DC, where the rest of my family was living. We joined the church my family was attending, which was the church we had visited during the summer and holidays as well as the church where I received the Holy Spirit.

I loved that church, and I loved the pastor. He had given me a Bible when I was twelve with a handwritten note: "Study to shew thyself approved unto God, a workman that needeth not to be ashamed, rightly dividing the word of truth" (2 Timothy 2:15). Talking about spiritual discernment—only someone full of the Holy Spirit with fire could possibly discern anything good in me. I was a complete mess. I was as angry as I could be. I never thought I'd someday study to show myself approved unto God. It's amazing how he saw something worthwhile in me even though I was a block of ice at the time. I still have that Bible.

The way I reunited with the man who would become my husband was so God ordained. Our mothers knew each other; they were pregnant with us at the same time. He and I had always known each other but had never had any kind of relationship. When my grandmother and I moved to DC, we lived with my aunt and my mother. One Saturday night, a dear friend asked me to go with her to a concert at the church a block up the street. I didn't want to go because it was something out of the ordinary; I normally went to my own church. However, I felt an unction, if you will, so I told her I'd go. That was the beginning of my learning how to follow the leading of the Holy Spirit. The proof is in the effects. I often tell anyone who will listen and especially young women that they should follow the prompting or leading of the Holy Spirit when they're beginning to feel the need or desire to be married. I tell them that the Word says, "Whoso findeth a wife findeth a good thing, and obtaineth favour of the LORD" (Proverbs 18:22).

I tell women that one reason they can't be found by potential husbands is that they're not in the places where those potential husbands are searching. I'm not talking about going to some club or inappropriate place to be found by a man.

When I walked in the church, the first person I noticed in the choir was the man who was to be my husband. *What in the world is he doing here?* I asked myself. I said to my friend, "I know him." Both of us had moved to DC after high school graduation.

After service, he greeted me. I introduced him to my friend. He asked when Bible class was. I told him on Tuesday. He came to our Bible class on Tuesday night in July 1967, and we've been together ever since. I told you the proof is in the effects.

If that hadn't been the correct thing to do, that is, following the leading of the Lord to do something different and attend the concert up the street, we wouldn't still be happily married after forty-six years. Yep. Forty-six.

We were engaged in March 1968. Right afterward, he was drafted. Something (which I would like to believe was the Holy Spirit) told me, *Don't get married now. Marry him when he comes back.* I was beginning to recognize the voice of the Lord. We wrote to each other daily and sent tapes to each other frequently. We still have all the letters and tapes.

He came home on April 11, 1970, and we were married on May 23, 1970. We had our first daughter one year later, April 11, 1971, which I thought was very interesting. Two years and three months later, we had our second daughter.

This book is about allowing God to break our hearts and about dying to self. I haven't lost focus of that. So let me share with you that there is a continual breaking after the Lord cracks our hard hearts for the first time.

Because I don't recall seeing many if any truly godly marriages, I had my own ideas about what a marriage should look like as opposed to what the Word said about marriage. Mind you, I did hear scriptural quotes about marriage: "Wives, submit yourselves unto your own husbands, as unto the Lord. For the husband is the head of the wife, even as Christ is the head of the church: and he is the saviour of the body" (Ephesians 5:22–23). Of course, the parts I heard most often emphasized was "Wives, submit yourselves unto your own husbands" and "For the husband is the head of the wife." Of course, those passages were most often quoted by men. I didn't hear very often—and when I did hear it, it was skimmed over very quickly—"So ought men to love their wives as their own bodies. He that loveth his wife loveth himself" (Ephesians 5:28).

I didn't see a whole lot of lovingkindness shown. I needed a clearer understanding about marriage. I felt there was much more to it than I had seen. Our marriage was good, but somehow, I felt it could have been better. Now that I look back, it seems I needed some more heart-breaking!

I recall reading that marriage was like Christ and the church

> Wives, submit yourselves unto your own husbands, as unto the Lord. For the husband is the head of the wife, even as Christ is the head of the church: and he is the saviour of the body. Therefore as the church is subject unto Christ, so let the wives be to their own husbands in everything. (Ephesians 5:22–24)

What I saw didn't remind me anything about the bride of Christ. I love the scripture that says, "Ask, and it shall be given you; seek, and ye shall find; knock, and it shall be opened unto you" (Matthew 7:7). I know the Word of God is true because "I sought the Lord, and he heard me, and delivered me from all my fear" (Psalm 34:4).

In the next chapter, you'll learn that God does answer prayer.

CHAPTER 6

Retreat—The God Encounter

I went on a retreat in 1993–94. The first night was like nothing I had ever experienced. Oh my gracious! I think everyone should get away from the hustle and bustle at least once a year to attend a conference or retreat. The retreat served me well. We were in the mountains where we didn't have the usual distractions—no TV, only the basics.

Families could attend it. Usually, retreats are for the women as if the men don't need any retreating. No offense, brothers—don't even get me started on that one! The men slept in one set of rooms and the women and children in the other. We had some breakout sessions and would all come together for the night sessions.

I liked that the chairs were in a circle unlike at church; that made a world of difference because everyone could see each other. It was a close, warm feeling, no pretense. If you felt like pretending, that didn't last because God's presence permeated the room. If you know anything about the Lord, you know that when you're in His presence, you're in awe of Him and surrender to Him. That retreat was another example of the Lord continuing to break my heart. Though it took place twenty-two years ago, I can still feel the presence of the Lord when I reflect on it.

Back to the marriage. I can't remember which session I embraced or what I heard that broke something in me concerning how I was to treat the man of God He had blessed me with. But when we got home, I couldn't do enough for him; I couldn't give him enough respect. It was a pure delight to do things for him. I must admit that our marriage wasn't even close to being a bad marriage because we've always known that the Lord designed us for each other, but neither of us had been taught how to honor and respect each other as the Word described it.

After the retreat, I looked at my husband in a whole different light. I didn't see him; I saw God. I revered him as a God man. I realized that honoring this God man was inclusive of my worship of God. I hadn't had a clear understanding of that before.

Exodus 33:20 reads, "And he said, Thou canst not see my face: for there shall no man see me, and live." I fell to the floor under the power of the Holy Spirit. I had my hands extended to heaven, and I saw a light shining down from heaven! It reminded me of Saul on the road to Damascus: "And as he journeyed, he came near Damascus: and suddenly there shined round about him a light from heaven: And he fell to the earth, and heard a voice saying unto him, Saul, Saul, why persecutest thou me?" (Acts 9:3–4).

I can hear you saying, "Believers don't persecute Jesus." Well, Dictionary.com defines the word *persecute* as "to annoy or trouble persistently." Let's face it; I'd think that taking forever to come to the knowledge of who Jesus really is and how He expects us to behave is annoying and troubling to Him! We have no reason not to know who He is or what He expects of us because we have everything we need at our disposal. Don't you agree?

When I experienced this Saul-like encounter, it catapulted me to a whole other place in Him. Yes, I knew Jesus, but the encounter helped me realize that I'd always have another realm to go in Him, that I'd always have something to learn about Him. There is no such thing as exhausting Him. I learned at the retreat that He was inexhaustible! So now, I don't get comfortable in any place in Him because I know I can go higher and deeper. Thank God for giving me a teachable spirit. "O the depth of the riches both of the wisdom and knowledge of God! how unsearchable are his judgments, and his ways past finding out!" (Romans 11:33).

Another scripture that comes to mind is,

> That Christ may dwell in your hearts by faith; that ye, being rooted and grounded in love, May be able to comprehend with all saints what is the breadth, and length, and depth, and height; And to know the love of Christ, which passeth knowledge, that ye might be filled with all the fullness of God. (Ephesians 3:17–19)

Whew! This is blessing me right now.

The illumination that came over me was almost unbearable but in a good way. It showed me even more of me and things I needed to improve on. For instance, as I consciously honored, adored, and revered God, I saw my husband, who is second after God in my life. At that moment, I received another level of respect for him, another level of honor for this man of God who indeed was deliberately behaving as a God man rather than just a man to whom I was married. He was behaving as the head of our home. As I think back to then and now, I'm evidently not the only one whose heart was broken by God; we were both transformed.

Unless we have a clear understanding of honoring God first, we will never be able to honor each other in God's way. We're still talking about the Lord breaking our hearts. When you get the picture, you'll realize that God breaking our hearts is very beneficial to us and those around us. When we allow Him to continue breaking us, getting those things out of our hearts that don't belong there, He fills us with the things that do. For instance, the nine fruits of the spirit: "But the fruit of the Spirit is love, joy, peace, longsuffering, gentleness, goodness, faith, meekness, temperance: against such there is no law" (Galatians 5:22–23).

Take this opportunity to see where you are for real this time with possessing these nine fruits. When you possess all of them, you will look just like Him! I realize the Lord is still working on most of us, but we should be cognizant of where we are so we'll know what He has fixed and what needs more work. We should at least know what area needs breaking.

Talk about happiness and peace in the home? I assure you that working on dying to the flesh will cause you to experience the kind of peace that is unexplainable.

Our Children

We had children by the time we attended the retreat, and we thought we had a pretty good handle on raising them. But the retreat enhanced our relationship with our children in addition to our marriage relationship. It made all our relationships better!

When your relationship with the Lord is strengthened, all your other relationships will improve. God taught us how to honor and respect our children even more. We realized they were the called of God, and we treated them as such even if they hadn't begun to walk in the things of God. I'm so glad the Lord heard my cry in my seeking Him more where our marriage was concerned. I sought for greater and better, and I found it just as the Word declared.

CHAPTER 7

Understanding Your Purpose

Once you come to trust God with your life, you then begin to fully realize your purpose.

I say often when I minister, "I know we believe that we're on earth to have fun and enjoy life." Let me be more specific. Most of us feel the most important things for us to accomplish in life are to get a good education, get married, purchase a big house, drive a fine car, raise a family, and hang with the who's who club. Not!

Is the aforementioned part of the abundant life Jesus was talking about when He said, "The thief cometh not, but for to steal, and to kill, and to destroy: I am come that they might have life, and that they might have it more abundantly" (John 10:10). Absolutely! However, the Word also admonishes us: "But seek ye first the kingdom of God, and his righteousness; and all these things shall be added unto you" (Matthew 6:33). When you place the kingdom of God first, your life becomes fail-proof.

"Then said Jesus to them again, Peace be unto you: as my Father hath sent me, even so send I you" (John 20:21). We

have been sent by Him as He had been sent by His Father
to do whatever He needs done on earth. Until this truth
becomes ingrained in our hearts and minds, we won't be able
to thoroughly comprehend why we're here. The abundant
life is doing the will of the Father. "For the Son of man is
come to seek and to save that which was lost" (Luke 19:10).
Our primary goal should be to do the same. I cannot stress
enough how important it is to come back to why we are here
in the first place. All the other stuff is just a whole lot of busy
work, programs, etc. We have so much going on now in the
body of Christ until most of us probably need to just stop, take
inventory of what we're doing, and delete those things that are
not a part of what God has called us to do. We will be rewarded
for those things He specifically called us to do, not what we
thought we needed to do because everyone else was doing it.

What Determines Our Purpose?

Our purpose on earth is determined by what has molded
us while we were growing up. How else could we minister to
those who cross our paths? It's most effective to minister from
our experiences rather than someone else's experiences or what
we read. I'm sure you've had opportunities to be ministered
to by someone you knew had been through what you're going
through. By the same token, I'm sure you've been ministered
to by someone who didn't have a clue but tried to come across
as if he or she did. Did you notice the difference?

God never intended for us to go through everything in life. That's impossible; we're not God, so we couldn't bear it! While we haven't gone through everything in life, we can relate what we have been through (we're talking about painful situations) to any issue someone is going through. I often let others know when I haven't experienced the specific issues they're dealing with, but I certainly can relate to pain, disappointment, and heartache. I haven't been through a divorce, so I can't know what that feels like, but I know plenty of people who have, so I can direct individuals to them.

God sometimes allows us to go through horrible situations so we can help others who have been or are going through the same thing. It's hard to get some people to understand that God saw what was happening to us as children; He witnessed all forms of abuse. People ask me how a loving God would allow such things. My answer is that He is preparing you for your purpose. It's a whole other book to dig and delve into why our loving God allows things to happen to us. "And we know that all things work together for good to them that love God, to them who are the called according to his purpose" (Romans 8:28).

There's no way I could have explained that to anyone if I hadn't allowed God to break my heart. Until everything that's not like Him is removed from your heart, you'll still have a whole lot of junk in it that He didn't mean to stay there.

Frustration of Purpose

The adversary tries to defeat your purpose and make you believe what God said about you is not true: "He who began a good work in me will be faithful to complete it" (Philippians 1:6). We need to be aware of what our purpose is on earth. People of God, each of us has a specific anointing, calling, and purpose. If you're not sure what yours is, ask Him; He will make it plain. Then, find counsel or someone who will assist you in walking in your calling. Never underestimate your purpose or deem your purpose less than anyone else's. When you walk in your purpose, you are obeying the will of the Father, which makes what you do for Him as important as whatever anyone else is doing.

Never allow anyone to make you think that if you're not in a pulpit holding a microphone or singing to a crowd, you're not as valuable to the kingdom. Maintain your confidence in God alone rather than depend on another. Look to Him for whatever you need to cause His plan for your life to be realized. If you depend on others, you'll constantly be frustrated and disappointed.

We are responsible to God for fulfilling our purpose; it's in our best interest not to allow anything or anyone to frustrate our purpose.

CHAPTER 8

The Mind of God

After the initial breaking of my heart, my mind began changing. Bishop Neal Roberson sings "My Mind Is Gone."

My mind is gone, my mind is gone.
The Holy Spirit done took my mind, my mind is gone.

I didn't think and reason the way I used to. I realized I had a long way to go, but I was happy to notice the great transformation in my thinking patterns. Instead of thinking the worst of everything and everybody, I was able to give people a chance rather than rushing to judgment. My hard, cold heart coupled with all the craziness locked up in my judgmental, opinionated mind was not a good combination for anyone intending to walk with the Lord. There's a reason the scripture says, "Let this mind be in you, which was also in Christ Jesus" (Philippians 2:5). "And be not conformed to this world: but be ye transformed by the renewing of your mind, that ye may prove what *is* that good, and acceptable, and perfect, will of God" (Romans 12:2). I thank God that with a renewed mind, I started thinking the way God thinks about everything!

The adversary doesn't care if you have made a shift in the way you think; he will still try to draw you back into thinking and behaving the way you used to. The key here is to recognize it when that happens and tell him,

> Then Peter took him, and began to rebuke him, saying, Be it far from thee, Lord: this shall not be unto thee. But he turned, and said unto Peter, Get thee behind me, Satan: thou art an offence unto me: for thou savourest not the things that be of God, but those that be of men. (Matthew 16:22–23)

Because of our sinful nature, we are programmed to sin: "Behold, I was shapen in iniquity; and in sin did my mother conceive me" (Psalm 51:5). We sin with our hearts and minds, but applying the scriptures rather than just quoting them affords us daily growth in Him. We must be very careful to take the things of God very seriously. God tells us, "Because the carnal mind is enmity against God: for it is not subject to the law of God, neither indeed can be. So then they that are in the flesh cannot please God" (Romans 8:7). We please God by obeying His Word and asking for forgiveness when we mess up. That can happen only if we allow Him to break our hearts. Believe me when I tell you it's an ongoing process.

CHAPTER 9

When You Love God for Real

When we love God for real, we will seek to keep His commandments. "If ye love me, keep my commandments" (John 14:15). No way will we be able to keep His commandments without possessing *agape* love, the love of Christians for others that corresponds to the love of God for all humanity. Agape love can come only from a broken and contrite heart. "The sacrifices of God are a broken spirit: a broken and a contrite heart, O God, thou wilt not despise" (Psalm 51:17). Yes, I know I've quoted this scripture before, but I cannot quote it enough!

Possessing the Holy Spirit with fire helped me cooperate with the Holy Spirit whenever He was prompting me to do something my flesh didn't feel like doing. The Word declares, "I indeed baptize you with water unto repentance. but he that cometh after me is mightier than I, whose shoes I am not worthy to bear: he shall baptize you with the Holy Spirit, and with fire" (Matthew 3:11). If you want your love to extend beyond what or how you feel, the baptism of the Holy Spirit with fire will do it!

Our *phileo* (physical or natural affection) love appears to be God's love. What is really sad is that most believers don't know the difference between man's love and God's love. Here is one way to differentiate. When someone mistreats you and you retaliate in any way, you don't have agape love. If you've done nothing to cause the mistreatment, it's God's way of giving you an opportunity to show whomever has mistreated you to be honest and share what's really wrong. Those with issues feel safe to let their hurts, disappointments, and pains out on someone they feel won't retaliate.

We must take advantage of this opportunity to teach them by example how to appropriately handle whatever mental anguish they may be going through. Let's remember that we didn't always know how to manage our feelings, emotions, and pain until God showed us how undone and sinful we were. It's our duty to teach by example and do what we can to help others when they cross our paths. Another reason why it's imperative that our hearts be broken and put back together by the love of God is so we can fulfill our purpose on earth. His love will help you realize that He is truly all you need, and when you have Him, no one or nothing else is needed.

He's All You Need

You know by now I have a song for every occasion. "Long As I Got King Jesus" was sung by Vickie Winans.

But long as I got king Jesus,

long as I got king Jesus,

long, long, long as I got Him,

I don't need nobody else.

You will experience ill treatment from in many cases those you'd least expect it from. I learned quickly to trust God and depend on Him alone. I found out through hardship, jealously, envy, and strife that as long as I have King Jesus, I didn't need anyone else. The love of God will cause you to be confident that you don't need anybody besides Him! Believe it or not, your experiences will allow you to be more effective because your confidence is in Him.

The loving way you respond to ill treatment lets God use you as an example of agape love. I believed the Word but didn't know how I could love someone who had misused me. When I had devastating experiences, I was amazed at how God healed my wounds, and I still am. I've experienced so many instances of craziness, but I won't share them because it would be to no avail. The Word of God works if you let it. If the Word says love your enemies, God will give you the power and the strength to do that.

Agape love is the love God commanded us as believers to have for everyone, believers or not. Agape love has nothing to do with how you feel but with doing what's right according to the Word. It has to do more with how you behave; you can show love whether you're feeling warm and fuzzy or not. Exhibiting love to others when they are showing you the opposite can oftentimes draw them to Christ. If they are believers, it will cause them to repent of their behavior. It's a beautiful thing to see the love of God transform someone right before your eyes.

At one time, we lived in a rough neighborhood, and there were several tough guys in our complex. One afternoon, we were on our way into our apartment and noticed that the ringleader of the group was sitting on the stoop. You could tell he didn't expect us to say anything to him since we had never spoken to him before. I'll never forget the expression on his face when my husband offered him a candy bar. All we had ever seen was a scowl on his face, but that day, he broke out with the prettiest, brightest smile I'd ever seen.

Sometimes, we have to get out of our comfort zone and express the love of God to others. These things can come only by cooperating with the Holy Spirit as it prompts us to be doers of God's Word and not hearers who deceive ourselves. "But be ye doers of the word, and not hearers only, deceiving your own selves" (James 1:22). It is and always will be a heart thing, and a heart thing has everything to do with the love of God.

CHAPTER 10

Worship Ready!

One of the most important things I learned since I allowed the Lord to continue breaking my heart is what worship truly is. The Holy Spirit continues to break this thing down for me, do you hear me? There's nothing like the Lord illuminating and opening His Word up to you. "God is a Spirit: and they that worship him must worship him in spirit and in truth" (John 4:24).

Jim Butcher, the pastor of Congregational Care and Counseling at Del Rey Church in Playa del Rey, California, says, "We need to worship with all of our spirit and worship in the truth of the Bible's teachings." Our worship should go beyond throwing up our hands for a couple of hours on Sunday morning. It's much more than singing the latest worship song or swaying in sync with the person next to you. The greatest worship we can give God is worshiping Him with all our spirit and in the truth of the Bible, the only truth.

Worshiping God entails many things, but I will only name a few. How we treat each other daily (especially those in our homes) is an example of worship. I've seen Christian folk baptized and filled with the Holy Spirit treat each other at home like animals—scratch that—worse than animals, and then go to church and "worship." Are you kidding me? It's important to treat everybody right in our homes and outside them. If God hadn't broken my heart and emptied me out, I would be living my Christian life the same way I've observed others behaving over the years. Am I judging? Of course not. I'm just observing.

I am a living witness that when Jesus Christ, the King of Glory, the Heart Breaker, gets hold of your heart, you won't know any other way to worship other than in Spirit and the truth of His Word. Precious hearts, God's Word is for daily application, not just for reading it to let others know we know scriptures and where they're found in the Bible. I often hear Christians, believers if you will, say, "I know the Word." But you know the word only to the degree you obey it. Anything short of living the Word is just quoting scripture. "And my tongue shall speak of thy righteousness and of thy praise all the day long" (Psalm 35:28). Worship is an everyday affair, not just on Sunday. "Seven times a day I praise you for your righteous laws" (Psalm 119:164). When we practice the Word of God—the Commandments—every day, that prepares our hearts and minds for worship. When we arrive at our place of worship, we are worship ready.

Prayer is a form of worship. It's not about how many times you pray, but the Word does admonish us to "Pray without ceasing" (1 Thessalonians 1:17). You must maintain a spirit of prayer. Being conscious of this truth will make you remain in a posture of worship because you don't want to come before the Father with unforgiveness in your heart or unconfessed sin. Have you ever wondered why our service most times is like climbing a mountain? It's because we come to worship with everything on our hearts and minds except Jesus! How can we worship Him if He's not in our hearts and minds?

Worship takes preparation—all week, all day. The Father would be so pleased with this type of pure worship. Can you imagine if everyone came prepared this way? If you have ever been in this type of service, you know what I mean. This kind of service is so seldom until you always remember you're blessed to be in accord with others when you worship with them.

What Happens with Pure Worship

Pure worship brings about many things including submission, healing, deliverance, liberty, humility, and obedience.

Submission

Submitting to God gives us the strength and power to resist the devil causing him to flee. "Submit yourselves therefore to God. Resist the devil, and he will flee from you" (James 4:7).

Healing

"Heal me, O LORD, and I shall be healed; save me, and I shall be saved: for thou *art* my praise" (Jeremiah 17:14). The

Lord gave me this passage when I was seeking Him concerning whether He was calling me to the ministry. I had gotten several prophecies in succession telling me that the Lord was calling me to preach and teach the Word of God. I was interested in preaching and teaching with only my lifestyle, not over a pulpit. So I petitioned God to make it unequivocally plain to me that I should adhere to the prophecies I had received.

In my basement one Saturday morning, He took me to Jeremiah 17:14–20. The words lifted from the page and formed themselves into the face of God. He looked me square in the face and asked, "Do you believe me now?" I whooped and hollered for I don't know how long. That was another life-changing encounter with the Lord. When you allow God to break your heart, He'll continue to fill you up with whatever you need to complete your kingdom assignment.

I'm sure God, not man, called me to the ministry. I know because He healed me that very day from doubt. God heals us physically, mentally, spiritually—whatever way we need. I love the ending of the verse: "for thou *art* my praise." God healed me from doubt and sealed the encounter with praise!

Deliverance

I marvel at the continual deliverance that comes from true praise and worship. Ever since He healed me from doubt, my mind automatically goes to two scriptures: "Many are the afflictions of the righteous: but the LORD delivereth him out of them all" (Psalm 34:19) and "And call upon me in the

40

day of trouble: I will deliver thee, and thou shalt glorify me" (Psalm 50:15).

Liberty

Liberation takes place in a service where there is pure worship. How could it not? "Now the Lord is that Spirit: and where the Spirit of the Lord is, there is liberty" (2 Corinthians 3:17). Everyone feels liberated—shackles break and chains fall off. I have been in services where I have received answers to questions that had been so complicated I didn't have words to articulate them. But the Spirit of God made intercession.

> Likewise the Spirit also helpeth our infirmities: for we know not what we should pray for as we ought: but the Spirit itself maketh intercession for us with groanings which cannot be uttered. And he that searcheth the hearts knoweth what is the mind of the Spirit, because he maketh intercession for the saints according to the will of God. (Romans 8:26–27)

I pray that you see the benefit of opening your heart to God. I mean really, since He already knows our hearts, wouldn't it make sense to consciously have them pure and clean? He'll search our hearts and find all other kinds of junk that shouldn't be there. If you've ever been in a situation where you could barely utter a word but God interceded for you, you know what I'm talking about.

Humility

Pure worship brings about genuine humility that comes when you recognize who God is and understand just how majestic and awesome He is. Though we're far from perfect, He says, "The Spirit itself beareth witness with our spirit, that we are the children of God: And if children, then heirs; heirs of God, and joint-heirs with Christ; if so be that we suffer with him, that we may be also glorified together" (Romans 8:16–17). We are joint heirs with Christ? Who can stand, sit, or lie prostrate in His presence and not be humbled? No one.

Obedience

We will feel compelled to obey the Word and the voice of God when He speaks to us. The presence of God brings about a yes response in our spirits—a yes to His will and a yes to His way. Here are lyrics (song by the gospel artist Shirley Caesar) that speaks to the "Yes, Lord" in us.

> I'll Say Yes Lord Yes
> I'll say yes Lord Yes to your will and to your way
> I'll say yes Lord yes I will trust you and obey
> When the Spirit speaks to me with my whole heart I'll agree
> And my answer will be yes Lord yes

Having learned submission, healing, deliverance, liberty, humility, and obedience to God helps me stay worship ready!

CHAPTER 11

Ministry

When the Lord spoke to my husband's and my hearts about beginning official ministry—I say official because we'd been doing unofficial official ministry behind the scenes for years—He gave us a dream the same night while we were vacationing in Florida. The gist of the dreams were that the Lord was calling us to build a church. Neither of us felt the call to build four walls, so we were trying to figure out how to build a church without walls.

The Lord made it clear to us that we were to build at least four people wherever we saw the need because inevitably those would be the people He was calling to lead His people. How in the world can you effectively lead people if your heart hasn't been broken by the Lord? "An unbroken heart leads to even more brokenness." I wholeheartedly believe that when we lead and minister out of our own pain, unforgiveness, bitterness, strife, envy, deceit, and jealousy, we transfer what resonates in us to others who have their own share of the same things.

We need to lead God's people from a place of a God-broken heart rather than from a heart of flesh. Flesh breeds filth and dirt. The Word says, "But we are all as an unclean thing, and all our righteousnesses are as filthy rags; and we all do fade as a leaf; and our iniquities, like the wind, have taken us away" (Isaiah 64:6). A God-broken heart breeds love and kindness: "The LORD hath appeared of old unto me, saying, Yea, I have loved thee with an everlasting love: therefore with lovingkindness have I drawn thee" (Jeremiah 31:3).

While having a birthday get-together for me at our daughter's home, she said, "We'd probably know what we were going to do if Mommy and Daddy went ahead and did what God told them to do." She probably to this day has no idea what an impact that statement made on our lives. That was the kick in the gut we needed to ask the Lord where, when, and how to begin our ministry.

I finally realized how much of an impact our obedience to God played in our children's lives. I knew we had to forge ahead no matter how much we didn't want to. Having learned about submission and obedience to God, I knew it was time to move. I'm reminded of another old song my grandmother used to sing, "You've Got To Move." I didn't understand it then, but I do now! The writer of the lyrics is unknown, but it was first recorded by the Two Gospel Keys in 1948, the year I was born. Someone said the song was about death, but I believe it can apply to believers in Christ moving upon hearing the voice of God in the direction He's calling them.

You've got to move you've got to move

you've got to move, child

you've got to move,

    but when the Lord Gets ready you've got to move.

Many times, we don't understand how much we hold our family members and the saints back by not understanding that what we do or don't do has an effect on their lives especially when we have been chosen as leaders. We help others realize their places in Him by being in the right place at the right time to meet whomever we need to meet to accomplish what God needs us to for His kingdom. My daughter's statement still hits to the core!

We began planning to do what we had heard the Lord tell us to do. We had to move! We had to build! In January 1999, I took a marketing assistant's position with a firm in Chantilly, Virginia, until my husband had done all the paperwork to begin our ministry. We took the plunge in June 1999 when my husband, our youngest daughter, and I began OWRAH Fellowship Ministries in Manassas, Virginia. On our way to the Best Western, the ministry's site, that Sunday morning, you would have thought we were going to be executed. We were happy to be starting but sad because we felt so inadequate. We knew a bit of what we'd face because we had been working behind the scenes in ministry for years doing whatever we could to help our brothers and sisters stay with God and obey leadership. We felt heavily burdened; I now realize we should have sought more support.

At times, God means for us to go it alone, but I don't think that was one. Though we felt burdened, nothing was wrong with our spirits or our joy in the Lord. I did praise and worship as if we had a full house. I often tell people that the Lord had us go through the ins and outs of beginning ministry so we would know how to help others not experience what we had.

As the Lord sent people to the ministry, we were encouraged, and momentum picked up as well. We faced some trying situations that again I wished we had handled differently. I thank God for the good sense to learn from our mistakes.

From the Best Western, the Lord made a way for us to lease space in Manassas. We were so grateful to have a place where we could do whatever we needed. The Lord allowed my husband to renovate the space pretty much by himself! The Lord blessed us mightily in that place.

Later, we relocated the ministry from Manassas to Culpeper, Virginia, since the majority of the saints lived there and in Harrisonburg, Virginia. My husband and I moved closer to our ministry; we felt everything was being directed by the Lord since He seemed to be in the purchase of our new home without a down payment or a job.

It was amazing how swiftly the Lord was moving. There was no time for doubt. Besides, the Lord had healed me of doubt. When we focus on our calling and purpose, He does the unimaginable. When we take care of ministry and His people, He simply makes a way out of no way. We've been in that home for fourteen years, and out of all of the houses we have lived in, it is the best. Our home is so flooded with the love of

God until sometimes my husband and I will look at each other and shake our heads because the peace of God permeates our dwelling. When people come for a visit, the first thing they say is, "Wow! This is so peaceful and warm." We usually have to either ask them to leave or invite them to spend the night. We finally realized, "Who in their right mind would want to leave the presence of God?"

This all came with a cost; nothing is free. We say salvation is free, and it is, but we have to pay to keep it. It takes sacrificing to do what is right rather than what our flesh dictates; we have to obey His Word. Absolutely nothing suits God but what He asked you to do! The best way to make it happen is to continue allowing Him to empty you out and fill you up with Him. You cannot do it on your own.

Back to how we got our house. The real estate agent called us about the house right when it went on the market. We went to look at it right away, liked it, and put a contract on it. We were told that another buyer was willing to pay cash as well as an additional $5,000. We were extremely blessed. I know we hear it a lot, but it bears repeating: "What God has for you is for you."

My husband had retired, and the company I'd been working for had closed. I was having the most difficult time finding suitable employment. But that didn't surprise me; I knew from experience that if the Lord doesn't want you to find work, it doesn't matter how many jobs are available, you won't find work. He's working on something else that needs immediate attention, and it's a way for Him to say, "Trust me." At times, the Lord wants to show His ultimate glory. If we had been working, we could say that we obtained this house because we had income and money for a down payment. But without employment, the world as well as the believers could see that and understand that only God could do this!

God heightened our trust even more. We learned how to trust Him by speaking His Word over situations. In August 2002, our youngest daughter began experiencing even more severe migraines, which she had been having since age thirteen. Due to all the medications, other parts of her body began to have problems and shut down. In December 2003, she was admitted to the hospital and placed in the ICU suffering from kidney failure. I wondered whether she'd make it. But the Lord reminded me that He had healed me from doubt. He brought her through miraculously! Even though she continued to suffer with migraines and was in and out of the hospital three or four times per week, we continued in our ministry as if we weren't in great mental and physical anguish. I believe we should experience God's Word as opposed to quoting what it says.

One of my favorite scriptures is Psalm 34; I had long since learned to "bless the Lord at all times" even when I was in so much physical and emotional pain that I didn't think I could catch my breath. Use your next breath to bless the name of the Lord! It also was a great comfort because I had learned how to worship God in Spirit and in the truth of His Word. I sang songs of praise and adoration to the Lord no matter how bad things were.

The trust comes when we continue what He's told us to do even though we're bombarded with trauma and drama. One of my husband's favorite sayings is, "When you take care of God's business, He'll take care of yours." It's true! None of these things could have taken place if I hadn't allowed the Lord to break me. People of God, I had an encounter with the Lord! I wouldn't be here to tell the story had I not.

We celebrated our fifth ministry/pastoral service in June 2004, which culminated OWRAH as we knew it. As far as disbanding, there was no such thing; since OWRAH Fellowship was birthed by us, nothing can be unbirthed.

From June 2004 on, we visited other ministries as the Lord led us and were told we were always right on time. Having lived through leading an intimate ministry, we knew firsthand the discouragement and weariness pastors can suffer. Unlike ministries already set in place by someone else, starting a ministry is nothing but work and more work with very little help from anyone. Unless you were sent out by a large church, you were totally on your own. You had no other source but God. I've learned that God makes the decision as to which route He will take you. Some pastors are called to step in behind someone else with everything already in place, while others are called to pave the way. I believe that whichever one God has called you to is equally as challenging.

Fast-forward to 2016. God has been exceptionally gracious and kind to us. June 2016 marks our seventeenth year in ministry. We never could have made it had God not broken my heart. I had to have been dead to self in order to have made it this far.

As we continue visiting and encouraging pastors and ministries, we come across people who need our help to get their lives in order and begin their ministries. It's vitally important to begin with a self-inventory to make sure you have done everything necessary to get straight first before trying to lead anyone else. Ask God to prepare your heart for ministry by breaking your heart and giving you His. Once your heart is emptied of you and filled with the love of Christ, you'll be in a position to lead His people. I'm a living witness that I (flesh) died when God broke my heart!

CHAPTER 12

Elevation

I believe that the higher we want to ascend in ministry, the lower we should go in humility. The higher we go, the greater our responsibility.

When I became an evangelist, I didn't clearly understand the call of an evangelist. Sure, I knew what the word *evangelist* meant—I was to support the pastor, preach the gospel of Jesus Christ, and spread the Word by being an example of Christ's love. But when I became a pastor, the gravity of elevation escalated. Having the responsibility for each sheep's growth and development in Him was a bit overwhelming. The posture of being a pastor was weightier than I had imagined. I still can't understand how He gives me the ability to deal with others according to who they are as well as their learning capability. When I truly understood this, I asked myself, *How in the world can leaders think of themselves more highly than they ought to think?* By the time you think you have others figured out and on the right track, their personalities, behaviors and everything else change. It's a full-time job and some.

Becoming an overseer took me to a whole other level. Lord, I thank you for breaking my heart and for allowing me the discipline to die to my flesh. Overseeing different ministries while having the responsibility of your own ministry is not for the easily flustered! The main thing to recall is that the people belong to God. With a clear understanding of that truth, you won't be so quick to throw up your hands and say, "I quit!" There is no quit in Him!

I am most grateful for the Lord making it plain to my husband and me who we are in the kingdom of God. Without a doubt, we know we are to hear and obey His voice when He tells us to go visit Pastor so-and-so today. As leaders, we can become discouraged at times. This is why it's so important to obey the Lord's prompting when He asks us to go see about one of His. Saying "I love you" is one thing, but showing up is much better. Seeing love speaks volumes. The Lord allows us to go through different experiences so we can teach others. Well, ever since He broke my heart and filled me back up with His love, I can do everything in my power to show others we should be even more loving and compassionate to those in leadership who have not yet experienced love in action.

Note to leadership: Let's support one another rather than compete with one another.

Since continuing to visit other ministries and encourage other pastors as the Lord directs, we have come to understand the proper name for what we were operating in is called parachurch ministry. The Greek prefix *para* means to be at the side of something; it's a name often given to Christian ministries that don't operate as churches but focus on one particular need outside the normal operations of a church.

Our specialty is developing leaders; we help them understand what needs fixing and assist them in fixing whatever is broken God's way. We need to address why our hearts are cold and stony. When we allow God's love to come in, it will break our stony heart and fill us with His love.

God's love cannot be undermined as man's love can. There is no deceit in God's love. As the Lord elevates us, let us be godly happy for our brothers and sisters in Christ. Since those of us in leadership understand the weightiness and the responsibility, why not sincerely pray for the success of each other's ministries? The higher He elevates us, the more love of God we should exemplify.

CHAPTER 13

God Did It!

My Parents Reunited in Marriage

Miracles continued to happen as I allowed God to break my heart. I want to share one of the greatest miracles. Thanks be unto God for the miracle of trusting Him no matter what it looked like and no matter how long it took for Him to answer.

The mysteries of God are astounding. My heart is full of gratitude for what He has done in my life. I'm forever amazed at His grace. His love and kindness, His patience with me while I was in my sinful, hard-hearted state is overwhelming. When I think about the miracles He performed, I just shake my head. Here are a few of them.

After I prayed about it for thirty-two years, God allowed my stepfather and my mom to remarry. He lived for two more years before he passed away leaving everything to my mom. I mention this because he always said that he would never get back with her or give her anything! When I ask myself, *Why on earth did I continue praying for them to be reunited when I didn't see any signs of this ever happening?* I never thought about this scenario in detail until now. I firmly believe it was because of my broken heart. As God continued to break my heart—emptying out me and filling me with His love, others saw Him instead of me. Am I tooting my own horn? Absolutely not! If I could only make you understand how incredibly undone I was and capable of anything bad you have heard or seen on the news.

One thing I learned some time ago is never tell or even suggest to anyone how good or how moral you are but how good He is! No matter what your status or title is, you are capable of anything anyone else is capable of (I'm referring to bad things right now). By the same token, you are equally capable of anything good with the help of the Lord.

Back to my mother and stepfather. In the summer of 1993, we relocated to Maryland and moved in with my stepfather. He was getting over prostate cancer, and we were having financial issues, so we decided we could help each other out. He progressed well as human beings normally do when they're happy. We genuinely enjoyed each other's company. I think it was the winter of 1995–96 that we had a snow storm that left us stuck in the house for a couple of days. One of those nights, we went for a ride in our Sidekick. While sitting in the backseat, my stepfather noticed my husband and me carrying on a conversation. He asked, *Do you talk to each other like that all the time?* We were baffled as to what he meant because we were just yapping away as we always did. After a few minutes, it dawned on us what he was really asking. He wanted to know if we spoke to each other in a loving tone and if we really enjoyed each other's company as it appeared we did. We told him yes we did. Did we ever get upset with each other? Yes indeed! We explained that the key was not yelling and screaming at each other. Whenever we could feel a "mad" coming on, we would stop talking until we could communicate respectfully.

I think my stepfather said to himself, *Maybe my wife and I can do this.* I'm not trying to sound humble. Trust me when I tell you that the Holy Spirit taught my husband and me how to do what we do. But first, he had to break us. The Holy Spirit is the best teacher I know. He will teach you how to do it the right way especially if it's an area where you haven't had many examples.

Not to bore you with the whole story, let's jump to when my stepfather called me and asked me how I would feel if he and my mom remarried! That was one of the happiest days of my life. It boosted my faith, trust, and love for God all the more. I whooped and hollered like a deranged woman. I felt such a huge relief. I was elated that I had obeyed the Lord and kept on praying about something I felt deep in my spirit would be accomplished for His glory. I'm confident their reunion gave hope to others in situations that seemed hopeless.

"Saints Don't Stop Praying" is another song we used to sing back in the day and I still sing today. It was written by the late Bishop G. E. Patterson.

Saints don't stop praying for the Lord is nigh
Saints don't stop praying He'll hear your cry
For the Lord has promised and His Word is true
Just don't stop praying He'll answer you.

I pray that my attempt to convey my gratitude to the Lord for the miraculous things He has done in my life has blessed you, especially the miracle of penetrating my heart when I didn't think that was possible. I still haven't gotten used to the pliable heart He has given me. At times, I'd like to feel that old hardness so I won't have to do some of the things He's asking me to do, but that thought lingers for only a moment. I wouldn't take anything for my journey now. I'm too close to turn back.

I hope you'll see the benefit of allowing the Lord to break your heart so you can experience His love. It has the power to get you through any situation. The Word says, "There is no fear in love; but perfect love casteth out fear: because fear hath torment. He that feareth is not made perfect in love" (1 John 4:18). We live in a time when there is much fear because we're not safe at school, on the street, in the mall, and not even in our homes or churches. "The safest place in the whole wide world is in the will of God" are lyrics of "The Will of God" performed by Karen Clark-Sheard.

Since I began this book approximately three years ago, many things have happened to me and to our family. My heart has been truly broken a few times to the point of saying to myself, *I'm not sure if I can take any more physical heartbreak.* But in spite of the physical, emotional, and spiritual heartbreak and disappointments I've endured, I'm even more convinced that the more we allow our hearts to be broken by God, the more we'll be shaped in His image. In these end-times, the only way souls can come to Christ is by seeing God demonstrated in our lives every day. The Word has not changed; He said if I be lifted up, I'll do the drawing. So let's stop lifting up ourselves (flesh), man, this, that, and the other. We've tried all that, and where has it gotten us? Wait. Don't answer that. That's another book!

By now, I hope you've decided to map out a plan to get your heart in order so when folk see you coming, all they will see is the all-consuming fire of God permeating your life. Your goal should be to intentionally be responsible for at least one soul per month by asking, "What must I do to be saved"? This happens most often when He has broken our hearts and (our flesh) has died.

About the Author

Overseer Dr. Priscilla H. Penn earned her Ph.D. in Religious Philosophy from Tabernacle Bible College and Seminary (TBCS), Tampa, FL. in 2007. She was ordained pastor into Mount Olive Kingdom Fellowship Covenant Ministries, Washington, DC in 2011 and on September 26, 2015 Dr. Penn was Appointed Overseer by Presiding Prelate Dr. Shirley Holloway.

In August 2015 she became a Certified Professional Coach, (CPC) with an earned certificate from the College of Social and Behavioral Sciences, (TBCS), Tampa, Florida.

A native of Danville, Virginia, Overseer Penn is Co-founder of OWRAH Fellowship Ministries. Since beginning the ministry the Lord called she and her husband to in 1999 in Manassas, VA, clarity has been brought to specify who they are in the kingdom of God. Thereby; they are leaders of a PARA-Ministry - instrumental in instructing and empowering individuals to pursue the plan of God for their lives.

Overseer Penn's track record as a prolific communicator and prophetic voice, has established her as one of the most respected leaders today. She is best known as a prayer warrior and a worship specialist who has a heart for obeying the voice of God.

She co-authored a book - "7 Ingredients To An Effective Prayer Life" - Book Series Volumes 1 & 2 - Compiled by Apostle Trena D. Stephenson.

In 2012 Overseer Penn toured Israel with her entire family and in 2014 she was blessed to minister in Lagos, Nigeria.

Among Overseer Penn's many accomplishments, she is extremely proud of her husband, Overseer Dr. Timothy H. Penn to whom she has been married for 46 years. She is a committed mother of three daughters, two grandchildren and a host of spiritual sons and daughters and live in Warrenton, VA.

Printed in the United States
By Bookmasters